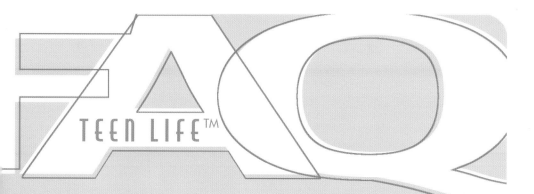

FAQ

TEEN LIFE™

FREQUENTLY ASKED QUESTIONS ABOUT

Loneliness

Robert
Greenberger

ROSEN
PUBLISHING®

New York

Published in 2008 by The Rosen Publishing Group, Inc.
29 East 21st Street, New York, NY 10010

Library of Congress Cataloging-in-Publication Data

Greenberger, Robert.
Frequently asked questions about loneliness / Robert
Greenberger.—1st ed.
   p. cm.—(FAQ: teen life)
Includes bibliographical references and index.
ISBN-13: 978-1-4042-1940-3
ISBN-10: 1-4042-1940-4
1. Loneliness in adolescence. I. Title.
BF724.3.L64G74 2007
155.5'182—dc22

                      2006039718

Manufactured in the United States of America

Contents

Introduction

There is a vast difference between being alone in a room and feeling lonely. The former is a temporary, perhaps voluntary situation that doesn't necessarily carry with it any impact, fleeting or lasting. Technology has allowed us to stay connected with friends and family, even when physically alone in a room or moving amongst strangers. You may be alone, yet engaged in conversation on message boards, in chat rooms, or via e-mail, text messages, and cell phones.

However, loneliness, as opposed to being alone, is an emotional state that people at all ages can feel, whether by themselves, with their romantic partner, hanging out with friends, or surrounded by a large crowd. It is an emotional state, not a physical one. It's a feeling of solitariness, isolation, and lack of warmth and love that is not necessarily dependent upon how many people are around you. Left untreated, loneliness can lead to other emotional and psychological problems. In fact, some studies indicate that a quarter of the United States population considers themselves lonely at any given time.

Loneliness is the awareness that you are not feeling connected to peers or family or the world around you. This can happen in overt ways such as being excluded from a group or feeling unloved by those in your social circle. You may feel alienated from your surroundings (either familiar ones or new ones). You may think that there is no one with

Everyone feels alone every now and then. However, when you're consistently lonely, even when you're around other people, you may need to seek the root of the problem.

whom you can or want to share your thoughts and feelings. You may sense that you are alone with no alternatives. When caught up in these kinds of emotions, try to remember that feeling a certain way isn't the same as being a certain way. You may feel alone, unloved, and without hope, but that doesn't mean you truly are alone, unloved, or without hope.

A Vicious Cycle

Several pioneering loneliness studies from the early 1980s found that lonely people describe themselves as feeling worthless, helpless, powerless, unacceptable, self-absorbed, separated from other people, nervous, empty, and disoriented. They can also feel boredom, self-pity, sadness, and depression. As a result of these feelings, their self-esteem may be low, and they may feel that there is no one with whom they can speak directly, honestly, and intimately. People suffering from loneliness may crave connection but at the same time avoid it, becoming victims of loneliness' characteristic tortured logic. Lonely people may feel that they are alone because no one wants to be with them, so they defensively resolve to reject people who they feel have rejected them or who they fear will reject them.

These studies concluded that lonely people are actually more rejecting of other people than other people are rejecting of them. So lonely people often remain lonely without realizing how to break the vicious cycle of loneliness—mainly by reaching out to others for help—or even how they have perpetuated that cycle.

The Physical Toll of Loneliness

At the same time as these studies were being published, doctors began reporting that the number of people suffering from loneliness was reaching epidemic proportions. This was something of a paradox given the growing ability for people to stay in touch with the help of technological advancements. Since that time, e-mail, the Internet, chat rooms, message boards, blogs, Web cams, cell phones, text messaging, and other wireless communication devices have allowed people to reach out and stay in contact with others at any time of the day or night. Nevertheless, record numbers of people are reporting a sense of loneliness and disconnection from others.

These feelings of loneliness can take a physical toll on people. In March 2006, the University of Chicago released test results indicating that men and women between the ages of fifty and sixty-eight who scored high on a measure of loneliness also had higher blood pressure. High blood pressure can lead to heart disease, the number-one cause of death around the world and number two in the United States. The study noted that the physical effects of loneliness-induced stress are cumulative and increasingly accelerated over time. The University of Chicago researchers found that chronic loneliness can increase blood pressure at the same rate that blood pressure is ordinarily reduced by treatments such as weight loss and physical exercise. This means that loneliness can undo any positive steps you take to reduce your blood pressure. It also means that in a more general sense and at any age, loneliness is placing stress on your body and compromising your health.

The "Unholy Trinity": Depression, Anxiety, and Loneliness

Other findings in the University of Chicago report indicate that loneliness can be a genetic trait, meaning that if someone in your family has suffered from loneliness, you may be more susceptible to it. In addition, those who are chronically lonely also tend to exhibit signs of chronic depression and anxiousness, dubbed the "unholy trinity" by the report.

Though loneliness, depression, and anxiety are distinct feelings, they usually feed off one another. When you feel one, you may very well experience the others.

These three can drag you into a downward spiral if you do not seek help. At the very least, try to overcome your sense of loneliness and isolation by reaching out to friends and family members and talking about what you're experiencing. Also consider seeking professional help from a therapist or psychologist. He or she can help you explore your feelings and what is causing them and give you concrete suggestions for how to alter the behavior and thought patterns that may be holding you back. If the psychologist suspects that your loneliness and depression are chemical in nature—the result of a chemical imbalance—he or she may be able to help you get prescriptions for medication that will restore the proper chemical balance and relieve your symptoms.

If you are experiencing suicidal thoughts as a result of your loneliness and/or depression, call a suicide hotline (check online or in the Yellow Pages) or 911 immediately. Then make an appointment with a professional therapist who will help you confront your feelings and find a way to address them in a more positive and effective way that will keep you safe and protect your health.

one

WHAT ARE THE CAUSES AND SYMPTOMS?

Despite the increasing "connectivity" made possible by advances in Internet technology and telecommunications, record numbers of people are now describing themselves as lonely. One reason for this is the changes in society over the last century.

During the United States' colonial and pre-industrial years, the majority of Americans worked on their own in relative isolation, often tending to their farms or rural businesses without much interaction with others. As the Industrial Revolution of the mid-nineteenth century changed the method of manufacture and transportation, people were drawn together in increasing numbers, forming larger communities. The nation's economic life shifted from the farms to the cities, as manufacturing and heavy industry eclipsed agriculture. People began to migrate from the countryside into the cities, where they were joined by a

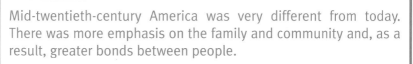

Mid-twentieth-century America was very different from today. There was more emphasis on the family and community and, as a result, greater bonds between people.

large stream of immigrants from Europe and Asia.

The new arrivals to the city—both the native-born rural Americans and the foreign immigrants—were often separated from their families. This often led to a sense of isolation and solitariness, even in the most densely populated of American cities. With family members now spread across the country, if not around the world, formerly close and emotionally sustaining connections began to grow more tenuous, and many Americans no longer received the basic nourishment that close personal and familial relationships provide. This trend deepened as both the nuclear (immediate) and extended families came under increasing stress beginning in the middle of the twentieth century due to suburbanization, divorce, two-career families, and increasing mobility and rootlessness. Indeed, 2000 U.S. Census figures show that 25 percent of the nation's households consisted of just one person, compared to 10 percent in 1950.

The Primary Relationship and Loss of Attachment

Dr. Robert Weiss, a pioneering sociologist at the University of Massachusetts, discovered in his studies that people lacking in primary relationships (that is, close friendships or romantic relationships) were often very lonely. As the divorce rate rose throughout the 1970s, Dr. Weiss noticed that as people dissolved unhappy marriages, the divorced individuals continued to feel lonely even after they formed new relationships and friendships. That ongoing lack of a "primary" relationship overwhelmed the amount of more casual interactions they might have.

A June 2006 study (not conducted by Dr. Weiss) in the *American Sociological Review* seems to back this up. It found that the average American had only two close friends with whom he or she could share and discuss important matters, down from an average of three in 1985. The number of people who said they had no such close friend rose from 10 percent in 1985 to nearly 25 percent in 2004. Almost one out of five people claimed to have only one close friend or confidante.

Dr. Weiss's studies led him to conclude that the removal of an "attachment figure"—no matter at what stage of life—will often lead to people feeling lonely. The attachment figure can be a caretaker, such as a mother for infants and best friends for adolescents. Their removal leads to feelings of emotional isolation. By age 17 or 18, some adolescents experience ambivalence (mixed feelings) about the severing of parental attachment as high school ends and early adulthood begins. Some teens are hesitant to form new attachments while there are remnants of the old ones.

Separating from Family and Old Friends

This kind of ambivalence can be observed earlier in adolescence, in junior high and high school, when more and more of a teen's emotional life is given over to school friends. As they become more attached to and emotionally dependent on their friends, many teens pull away from their parents and even shut them out of their personal lives. The straining or severing of such a fundamental tie—although it's a typical part of a teen's development process—can create a sense of loneliness. This can feel disorienting because you may want to be close to your friends and create some distance between you and your parents, but you find that your friends can't give you everything you need. Something is missing. That something is probably the profound, old, and very strong emotional tie that you have to your parents and will probably always continue to have.

Just as moving to a new neighborhood and school system may bring about a sense of loneliness, the first year of college can also be a difficult and isolating period of adjustment and transition. This can be particularly surprising because throughout your teen years, you are led to believe that college will be so much better than high school. You will have more freedom, more friends, more choices, and more fun. The expectations the student and others place on the college experience may set some people up to feel lonely when the reality doesn't meet the expectation.

10 FACTS ABOUT
LONELINESS

1 There is a vast difference between being alone and feeling lonely. The former is a temporary, perhaps voluntary situation that doesn't necessarily carry with it any impact, fleeting or lasting. Loneliness is an emotional state that people at all ages can feel whether by themselves, with their romantic partner, hanging out with friends, or surrounded by a large crowd. It is an emotional state, not a physical one.

2 Loneliness is the awareness that you are not feeling connected to peers or family or the world around you. It's a feeling of solitariness, isolation, and lack of warmth and love that is not necessarily dependent upon how many people are around you.

3 Some studies indicate that a quarter of the United States population considers themselves lonely at any given time.

4 Studies show that lonely people describe themselves as feeling worthless, helpless, powerless, unacceptable, self-absorbed, separated from other people, nervous, empty, and disoriented. They can also feel boredom, self-pity, sadness, and depression.

5 In March 2006, the University of Chicago released test results indicating that men and women between the ages of fifty and sixty-eight who scored high on a measure of loneliness also had higher blood pressure. High blood pressure can lead to heart disease, the number-one cause of death around the world and number two in the United States.

6 The University of Chicago researchers found that chronic loneliness can increase blood pressure at the same rate that blood pressure is ordinarily reduced by treatments such as weight loss and physical exercise. This means that loneliness can undo any positive steps you take to reduce your blood pressure.

7 Other findings in the University of Chicago report indicate that loneliness can be a genetic trait, meaning that if someone in your family has suffered from loneliness, you may be more susceptible to it.

8 Those who are chronically lonely also tend to exhibit signs of chronic depression and anxiousness.

9 A June 2006 study in the *American Sociological Review* found that the average American had only two close friends with whom to share and discuss important matters, down from an average of three in 1985. The number of people who said they had no such close friend rose from 10 percent in 1985 to nearly 25 percent in 2004.

10 The same study found that almost one out of five people claimed to have only one close friend or confidante.

Transferring to a new school or going off to college can be one of the loneliest experiences you'll face. However, this change can bring you new friends and experiences.

The reality is that college will probably be the first time you are away from your family and close friends for an extended period of time. The notion of starting all over again in forming bonds of friendship can overwhelm some people. Suddenly you will be a stranger again and may know no one, something you might not have experienced since kindergarten. You may no longer be part of a tight, supportive group of friends who have a long, shared history together. This sudden removal from the familiar and comfortable may lead to a sense of disconnection and loneliness. This loneliness can be intensified if your boyfriend or girlfriend goes to a different college or is still in high school. This means you will also be dealing with a long-distance romantic relationship. You will probably miss the person terribly—someone you previously saw and spoke to every day—and the distance and absence place a strain on the relationship. You may feel lonely despite living in a dorm full of sociable people.

Symptoms and Warning Signs

People who are suffering from loneliness exhibit several symptoms that may serve as warning signs. Observable indications of loneliness in a person can include low self-esteem and frequent bouts of anger or fear. They can also include harsh self-criticism, over-sensitivity to other people's criticisms or suggestions, and self-pity. The lonely person may also "act out" by being critical of others or placing blame on other people for his or her condition.

A lonely person can become easily discouraged or lose his or her usual interest in other people, places, or objects. This is

The anger that results from loneliness can damage relationships, leading to isolation and further loneliness. This increased loneliness, in turn, can lead to more destructive anger.

similar to depression, when people lose their passion for things they previously loved. A lonely person may avoid new experiences and as a result become isolated from peers and potential new friends. Some will actually do the reverse: to compensate for being lonely, they will reach out and become involved with activities or people without necessarily understanding what they have committed themselves to, who they are dealing with, what sort of time and energy will be required, and how genuinely interested in that activity or person they really are.

If left unacknowledged, unaddressed, and untreated, loneliness can lead to several more severe emotional health conditions such as depression, alcoholism, or drug abuse, all of which can result in serious physical health problems. In younger children, loneliness can lead to antisocial and self-destructive behavior. For teens, it can result in delinquent behavior, the abandoning of friendships, emotional separation from family members, learning and memory problems, neglect of schoolwork, and even dropping out of school.

So if you are feeling lonely, and you have been for a while, get help. Start by reaching out to a good friend or close family member. If you feel like you still need more assistance, perhaps from an objective person you are not so closely bound to, visit a therapist and work together to find your way out of your loneliness.

WHY AM I DEPRESSED?

Teens often feel lonely and/or depressed. It's a perfectly natural part of the maturation process. Loneliness can often lead to depression, and loneliness can be a symptom of depression. Lonely people, though, are not necessarily depressed, and the conditions can be easily confused. Depression manifests itself as withdrawal, anxiety, lack of motivation, and sadness. All of these symptoms closely mirror loneliness. While loneliness can usually be treated through counseling or various self-help strategies and techniques, depression often requires more intensive therapy and/or medication, depending on the depth and severity of the problem.

How Loneliness and Depression Differ

The most noticeable difference between loneliness and depression may be the way in which the sufferer reacts to

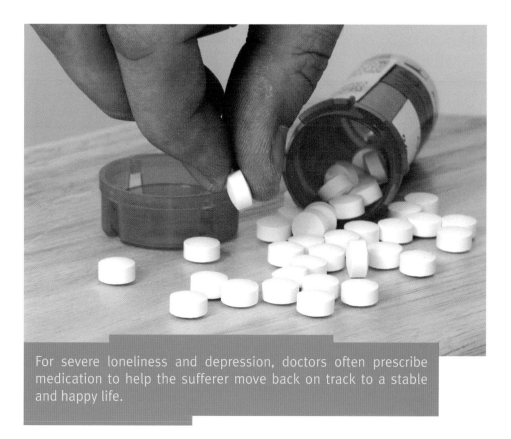

For severe loneliness and depression, doctors often prescribe medication to help the sufferer move back on track to a stable and happy life.

the condition. Dr. Robert Weiss, a sociologist at the University of Massachusetts, compares the two typical reactions: "[I]n loneliness, there is a drive to rid oneself of one's distress . . . [I]n depression, there is instead a surrender to it." Studies have shown that lonely and depressed people feel hopeless in equal numbers, and both groups are susceptible to suicidal thoughts and aggressive behavior. On the other hand, feelings of shame and guilt are more closely associated with depression. A 1979 study showed that depression, unlike loneliness, was categorized by anger and dissatisfaction with nonsocial aspects of a person's

Myths and Facts
About Loneliness

Loneliness is a sign of weakness or immaturity.

Fact ➤ Loneliness is a normal condition experienced by as many as 25 percent of the population (of all ages) at any one time. It is a problem reported by more and more people every year. A June 2006 study in the *American Sociological Review* found that the average American had only two close friends with whom to share and discuss important matters, down from an average of three in 1985. The number of people who said they had no such close friend rose from 10 percent in 1985 to nearly 25 percent in 2004. Almost one out of five people claimed to have only one close friend or confidante.

Loneliness is a harmless emotional "mood."

Fact ➤ In its most severe forms, loneliness is considered a serious, even life-threatening condition, one that increases the risks of heart disease and depression.

 Loneliness will pass if you just cheer up and "get out there," meet new people, and hang out with your old friends. Fact ➡ While it is a good idea to fight loneliness aggressively by trying to stay connected to other people, simply seeking out company will not solve all your problems. As John Powell, a psychologist at the University of Illinois counseling center, says, "The frequency of contact and volume of contact does not necessarily translate into the quality of contact." You need to be careful about how and with whom you try to find a connection. Many lonely people throw themselves into harmful friendships, romantic relationships, or sexual encounters simply to feel less alone. Try to form a connection to—or reconnect with—someone who is kind, trustworthy, stable, and genuinely cares for your well-being. Form a quality connection rather than something that is merely convenient or temporary.

 Loneliness is only a problem for old people, divorced people, or only children. Fact ➡ Anyone, of any background, at any age, for any length of time, can feel lonely, isolated, and disconnected from their lives, family, and friends.

People in romantic relationships never feel lonely.

Fact ➡ Everyone feels lonely at various points in their lives, even people with boyfriends or girlfriends. Even many married people often report feeling consistently lonely. Just as you can feel lonely and isolated in a crowd or within a big family, you can feel lonely when in an intimate relationship. You can feel temporarily disconnected or remote from your partner. Seeking a boyfriend or girlfriend only to dispel loneliness is a bad idea. It could make you act unwisely, choosing someone who is not truly a good match for you. You should enter a romantic relationship only when you really like someone, you have a lot in common, you are treated well, and you want to treat the other person well and share your good feelings with him or her. You can't simply look to a person to make you feel better. Only you can do that in the long run; it is your job.

Feeling lonely means you are alone. Fact ➡ Loneliness is a feeling. It is a feeling of isolation and aloneness. But feelings do not always correspond to reality. If you feel lonely, it does not mean you are alone. In fact, lonely people, fearing rejection, tend to push people away who are ready and willing to help. You have family members who want to help. You probably have friends who want to help. You have teachers and guidance counselors who want to help. All of these people want to listen to you talk about your feelings and concerns and try to offer advice and support. In addition, doctors, counselors, and therapists know exactly how to address the problems of loneliness, and they will do so with great compassion, understanding, and care.

life. Loneliness, however, was characterized by a low occurrence of social interaction, while depressed people were less reluctant to join social gatherings.

Depression is also something that can be more common and pronounced in certain seasons, occurring most often during the winter months. Loneliness, on the other hand, tends to be a more constant state. Nevertheless, people can function in a depressed state for an extended time. If the condition persists or gets worse, then medical help is called for. This is what is called clinical depression, indicating that the person's ability to function in society has been strongly affected.

A study conducted using the University of California, Los Angeles (UCLA) Loneliness Scale, the Belcher Extended Loneliness Scale (BELS), the Beck Depression Inventory, and patient questionnaires about social and emotional loneliness helped further delineate the differences between depression and loneliness. The main differences between the two conditions were broken down into four main categories. The first was the

> Social behavior is frequently affected by loneliness. People who feel isolated are often on the margins of the crowd, both voluntarily and involuntarily.

relative focus and scope of one's dissatisfaction. Lonely people tend to be dissatisfied with interpersonal issues, whereas depressed people are more often unhappy with matters on a wider scale. Second, the duration of the patient's feelings can help distinguish loneliness from depression. The longer the feeling has been in place, the greater the likelihood the condition is depression. The third distinguishing characteristic would be the feeling of guilt, which is more often associated with depression than loneliness. Finally, depressed people tend to develop more secondary disorders than lonely people do, including eating disorders (generally overeating or undereating), sleep disorders (such as insomnia), and alcohol abuse.

Those who suspect they are suffering from either loneliness or depression or perhaps both should immediately seek help from friends and family and seriously consider going to see a therapist. Left untreated, loneliness can turn into depression and

Finding the motivation to seek help for loneliness and/or depression might be one of the hardest things to do for the sufferer, but it is often the most important.

can result in a wide range of self-destructive and potentially dangerous behaviors. Don't hesitate to seek and accept help. Let people guide you out of the loneliness within which you feel isolated and trapped. Should you be a friend helping a lonely or depressed person who does not seem to be improving, encourage him or her to get professional help.

three

HOW DO I OVERCOME LONELINESS?

Coping with loneliness requires strategies that can be tailored to your particular lifestyle and circumstances. The first step is to recognize that loneliness is a very serious problem, and a very treatable one at that. Next, remind yourself that you haven't always felt lonely, so your current sadness and pain will pass; it is not forever. But you can't simply passively wait for your loneliness to pass. You must take action. You have to take personal responsibility for your situation. You have to take active measures to get "un-lonely," and looking for someone to do the work for you won't solve the problem.

Loneliness Doesn't Define You

Medical professionals, counselors, and psychiatrists offer a variety of strategies to help manage loneliness and eventually conquer it. They often recommend that you start by not allowing loneliness to define you. When you try to describe who you are, resist the tendency to identify yourself simply and reductively as "a lonely person." What other qualities do you have and how can you build on them? Are you creative? An artist? A writer? Are you athletic? A runner? A football or soccer player? A skateboarder? A bicyclist? Are you a caring, sympathetic person? Are you a reader? A science enthusiast? A nature lover? Try to refocus on what you're interested in, what you have a passion for, and who and what you love, and then remind yourself that these, too, make you what you are. Loneliness is only a small and temporary part of the entire picture.

An Action Plan

Experts also suggest you make a personal action plan to end your loneliness. Once created, you need to remind yourself in order to stay on track and follow through on the plan. If you're uncertain what form the plan should take, start by taking what is called a self-inventory. Quite often, loneliness can be brought about by a crisis of confidence or a diminished sense of self. Ask yourself what changes you want to make to your lifestyle, personality, appearance, and attitude to help put the loneliness behind you and make you feel better about yourself, more like the person you want to be. Examine the circumstances that led to the feeling of loneliness and then determine which elements should be changed.

Participating in community activities such as sports is often more effective in getting rid of loneliness than therapy and medication.

Get Involved and Reach Out

To help break out of the isolation that comes with loneliness, try to find ways to get involved with people and activities. However, do not just throw yourself blindly into relationships with people or into groups that you don't have a genuine interest in. This may lead to regrets, resentment, and a renewed sense of isolation and alienation from others. Remind yourself of your interests and passions and try to find like-minded people or activities that will allow you to pursue your interests. For example, you can join an after-school activity, club, or sport. Most schools offer a wide range of athletics, music and art classes, and clubs related to debating, politics, computers, science, photography, drama, media communications, and other fields of interest.

During the school day, classrooms offer an opportunity to speak to new people, as does the lunchroom, where you can try sitting at different tables. It's surprising how few people in your class you may speak to day to day. You may have been in all the same schools as another classmate for almost twelve years, yet rarely or never have spoken to him or her. Try identifying some people who have always seemed nice and interesting to you but, for whatever reason, you've never spoken to or befriended. Try striking up a conversation with them and see if you have any common interests or connections.

Wherever you are, you can find new situations and opportunities to expose yourself to and meet new people. Think about what interests you the most—baseball, football, soccer, yoga, Pilates, music, museums, Renaissance festivals, dancing, acting,

By involving yourself in more community activities, your confidence will grow to the point where you'll be able to spend time alone now without feeling your former loneliness.

comics and graphic novels, computers, movies, drawing, writing, role-playing games, surfing, radio broadcasting, etc.—and see if there are local organizations to join or activities to participate in related to your interests.

Places such as the community college or YMCA or YWCA frequently offer classes in various disciplines. Your local town or city hall or municipal building should have lists of community organizations and activities. Many localities have community or regional theaters that are often looking for volunteers for everything from set design and painting and costume management

Volunteer programs that involve teamwork are a great way to feel like you're part of the community. Everyone who participates is essential to the project and openly welcomed.

to lighting, sound design, and acting. Speaking of volunteering, every community is in great need of volunteers in hospitals, nursing homes, soup kitchens, shelters, after-school programs, tutoring centers, churches, and other institutions and programs. By signing up and getting involved, you can be doing something good for both yourself and your community. By helping others, you improve your feeling of self-worth, and you're usually working alongside other volunteers, getting a chance to reconnect and reintegrate yourself with the world around you.

Connectivity

If you have difficulty finding these kinds of opportunities, get on the Internet and search for events and clubs related to your interests and in your area. There may even be online groups and chat rooms devoted to some of your interests. These can be great opportunities to discuss some of your passions and talk to people who share similar interests and outlook.

Be careful, however, in coming to rely too heavily on the Internet "community" as a substitute for face-to-face interaction with other people. Loneliness can, in part, involve a sense of physical as well as emotional disconnection from other people. Face-to-face interaction can often be more emotionally satisfying and enriching than more remote contact, such as over the phone or Internet. Something often feels like it's missing when most or all of your communication is electronic, even if you are phoning or e-mailing or instant messaging a close friend. Another person's physical presence before you creates a greater sense of emotional intimacy and makes for a more satisfying, sustaining interaction. As useful a tool as the Internet has become, it can also become a crutch to avoid the real world. Recognize this and limit your online time each day. Use it as a reference and directory tool, not as a virtual community or circle of friends. Make it one part of your action plan, not the whole plan.

When you find an event to attend or a group to join, you should practice your social skills, which may be rusty. You can "warm up" by hanging out with a friend you may not have seen in a while. You can even think up and practice some conversation openers.

With social networking sites such as MySpace growing more and more popular, the Internet, if used responsibly, is a great place to meet new friends.

Each new person you meet and talk to is a new opportunity for friendship and connection. Don't worry if you don't feel any sense of connection after your first few tries. You won't necessarily click with everyone. But sooner or later, you will meet someone whose company you enjoy, who shares your interests and outlook, and who makes you feel less alone in the world.

Non-Romantic Forms of Intimacy

Once new relationships begin, don't forget that growing intimacy, whether platonic (friendship only) or romantic, takes time. In your eagerness to dispel your loneliness, try not to rush or force things. Putting too much pressure on a new acquaintanceship too early may prevent it from forming into an enduring friendship.

If your loneliness is mainly a result of the end of a breakup with a boyfriend or girlfriend, remember that a close friendship may be all you need at this time to help ease your sadness and isolation. Not every new relationship has to be a romantic one, even if you feel lonely because of a romantic loss. It is better to get back on an even keel and rediscover your happiness before you venture back into the dating world. Asking or expecting a new boyfriend or girlfriend to chase away your sadness and loneliness and make everything better is unrealistic and unfair. It will put far too much pressure on the relationship and the other person. Your happiness must bubble up from within; it can't be provided for you by someone else. Hold off on dating until your happiness is restored and you are able and ready to share that happiness with someone else. In the meantime, let friends and family members give you the emotional support, sympathy, and understanding you need.

Alone, but Active and Engaged

When you are struggling with loneliness and trying to put it behind you, it is important to reach out to friends and family members for help and companionship. That doesn't mean, however, that you must always be surrounded by people. It's OK to be alone while you're fighting loneliness. Sometimes you may not feel up to social interaction, and that's fine. The important thing is to avoid falling into a habitual avoidance of social situations. In addition to resting and recharging, you can use time spent alone to your best advantage. You can still pursue your interests independently of others, whether it's attending a play, reading a book, or enrolling in martial arts classes. In fact, staying active will help keep you stimulated and prepare you for the time when you feel more ready and able to reach out to others.

Even if you're not yet ready to be out and about in public, it is always a good idea to engage in some physical activity, be it a walk around the block, a bike ride, a yoga class, or a workout at the local gym. Exercise can be a natural mood enhancer, helping to lift your spirits and make you feel stronger, more in control, and more optimistic. Make sure you look after your nutrition and general health as well, including getting a proper amount of sleep so your energy levels, mood, and mental abilities remain strong. You should try to stick to a diet rich in fruit, vegetables, and proteins and low in fat and empty calories (such as soda, candy bars, and snack cakes).

Pets

Another option as you prepare to transition from isolation to engagement is getting a pet such as a dog or cat. According to the Centers for Disease Control and Prevention, there are a number of health benefits associated with pet ownership. In addition to easing feelings of loneliness, having a pet is associated with lowered blood pressure and decreased levels of cholesterol and triglycerides (a compound of fatty acids). And there is nothing quite like the unconditional love and affection pets can offer you every day.

However, owning a pet is a major undertaking that requires careful consideration. A pet should not be an impulse purchase. You should get a pet only if you want to love and care for an animal, not just to make yourself feel better. Being a pet owner is a serious responsibility. It is a life you are caring for and sustaining, and you must keep its best interests at heart no matter how badly you are feeling. If you've never owned a pet before, it's probably best to wait to get one until after you feel like you're on a more stable footing.

Getting Professional Help

There is always a possibility that what you're experiencing may be medical in nature. If you've tried all the techniques suggested here over an extended period of time and there is no real improvement, then you should consult with both a doctor and a therapist. These professionals can guide you through diagnostic

Pets, especially dogs, are often a welcome addition to one's life. Great friendships develop between people and their animals, which can help alleviate loneliness.

Ten Great Questions to Ask When You're Asking for Help

1 Is feeling lonely normal?

2 Is loneliness typical for someone my age? Does it mean I'm immature?

3 Do I feel lonely because I'm unlovable and no one wants to be around me?

4 Loneliness feels a little like depression. Am I depressed? How do loneliness and depression differ?

5 Can loneliness turn into depression?

6 Should I seek counseling for my loneliness?

7 Will loneliness get worse if I don't seek professional help?

8 Will loneliness have long-term effects on my physical or emotional health?

9 Is loneliness often treated with medication? If I do take medication prescribed by a doctor or mental health professional, will I need to for the rest of my life?

10 What are my options if my loneliness persists even after reaching out to friends and family members and visiting a therapist? Will this ever go away?

tests and exams that will help determine if there is a physical, chemical, or emotional issue that can be treated. If the problem is identified as medical—such as clinical depression or a chemical imbalance—then you can receive the appropriate treatment. You will also be reassured that you did your best dealing with it on your own, but that this was a problem that no amount of your own effort would solve. It required professional assistance, which is no different than seeking medical help for an injury or for chronic pain.

Never lose sight of the fact that it's perfectly OK to seek professional help. While you may feel alone and isolated, you are not the only one who feels that way. Ironically, many people feel alone and isolated. In fact, most people feel that way at least once in their lives. You may feel like you're alone, but you're actually part of a large "club." In many respects, everyone feels alone to varying degrees and at various times. Loneliness is an

Seeking professional help for your loneliness does not mean you are giving up, and it should not embarrass you. It is one of the most effective ways to address your problem.

extremely common feeling. But that doesn't make your pain and sadness any less real or important, and you should seek help for it. School counselors, doctors, therapists, religious leaders, and others have been trained to provide help or point you in the right direction to get the treatment that will be right for you.

If you're unsure whether you should just deal with this yourself and try to ride it out or get outside help, keep in mind that if you do not address the problem, it could get worse. Loneliness that is not addressed and treated effectively can lead to desperate attempts to solve the problem in counterproductive ways, such as alcohol and drug abuse, risky sexual activity, and binge eating. Whatever relief you may derive from such counterproductive coping mechanisms will be temporary in nature, will probably leave you feeling lower than before, and will not address the root causes of your loneliness. You will not gain any ground on your loneliness; you will probably end up losing ground.

At that point, someone may begin to contemplate even more desperate measures such as suicide. You must seek help before you arrive at this very dangerous and destructive path. If you are experiencing suicidal thoughts, get help immediately. Call a suicide hotline (look in the Yellow Pages or online), 911, or even a friend. Do not act on the impulse. Talk to someone, preferably a mental health professional or counselor, as soon as you begin to have suicidal thoughts. You are no longer in a position to be able to solve the problem all by yourself. Remember, loneliness will pass, but you will never be able to get your life back if you end it.

The Healing Process

Breaking free of loneliness is a process, sometimes a long one. But it takes just one step to get started. That first step may be finding one person to be your confidant and simply opening up to him or her. Let that friend know you're feeling lonely and need someone to talk to as you work your way through it. If he or she is receptive, then open yourself up gradually, establishing mutual trust and accepting your friend's advice if it seems sound.

Friends can become a sort of personal coach and encourage your step-by-step progress, even if they are not always at your

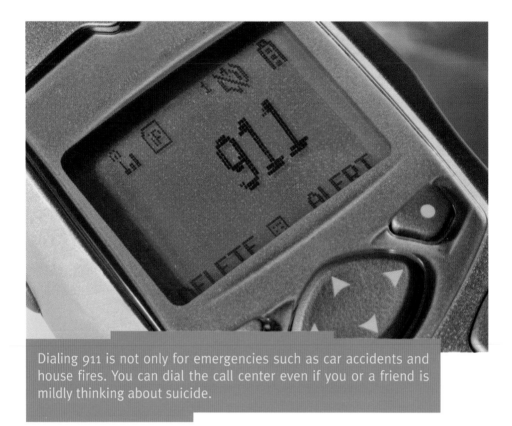

Dialing 911 is not only for emergencies such as car accidents and house fires. You can dial the call center even if you or a friend is mildly thinking about suicide.

side when you venture out and try new activities. If a friend knows what your goals are, he or she can be there to encourage you to forge ahead when you begin to get cold feet or yield to sadness and solitariness. It also allows you the opportunity to listen to your confidant's perspective, see the world through another set of eyes, and see yourself as other people see you. All of this can be helpful in breaking the cycle of loneliness, isolation, depression, and low self-esteem.

All of the strategies for coping with and dispelling loneliness discussed here require not only energetic commitment and perseverance, but an investment of time as well. Allow time for things to develop and your emotions to stabilize. Do not expect your loneliness to vanish the first time you sit at a new lunch table, try a new activity, or meet with a therapist. If something isn't feeling right or you remain feeling isolated after a good, sustained effort, then move on to another strategy. But the key is to be patient. Just as it took time to recognize you were lonely, it will take time for you to emerge from loneliness. One day you will realize that you feel happy and reconnected to the world around you.

four

HOW DO I HELP
A FRIEND WHO
IS LONELY?

Within your social circle, you may notice some mood or behavior changes in one of your friends. He or she may have stopped hanging out with the group or has begun making self-critical comments. Teachers, guidance counselors, parents, and other adults may notice the changes as well. The question then becomes, how can you help a person in need?

Teachers are trained to look for signs of trouble, but friends can notice the same signs more quickly. These include the person appearing sad, timid, anxious, or unsure of him- or herself for an extended period of time. Your friend may show a lack of interest in his or her surroundings or may have begun to isolate him- or herself in various social situations at school—from homeroom and lunchroom to gym class and after-school gatherings, always remaining apart and alone.

Peer Support

In some schools around the nation, principals are taking it upon themselves to track their students' social development as well as their academic progress. When it became clear at these schools that some students—the so-called nerds—were being isolated, marginalized, and, in some cases, picked on, the schools began a series of after-school activities aimed at their interests, such as chess and computers. This way, teens with similar interests could be brought together to form their own community, ending their isolation within the school.

In some of these same schools, social workers began weekly lunch groups where both shy and outgoing students were brought together for a chat, showing how much previously unexpected common ground existed between them. It was always there, just waiting to be discovered and unlocked. All it takes is one person reaching out to talk to another person and trying to make him or her as comfortable as possible socially.

If you feel like your friend or a fellow student is suffering from loneliness and needs help, alert a teacher or another responsible adult. This isn't being a busybody or a snitch. This is all about getting someone the help he or she needs before a problem can get much worse and more dangerous. School principals note that fellow students are able to identify loneliness in their peers about six weeks earlier than most teachers. If students can be enlisted to help administrators identify and offer help to those at risk or suffering from loneliness, a six-week jump on the problem can make a huge difference, possibly preventing the loneliness from

Close friends are often the most important people in the lives of those who are experiencing loneliness. Just being there can help significantly.

deepening and taking strong root. Teachers, guidance counselors, coaches, and religious leaders can work with lonely teens on an individual basis or share their observations with the parents to determine the best course of action.

Dr. Jerry Pounds, a professor of youth education in New Orleans, says, "Academically, teenagers tutoring other teenagers has become both popular and helpful. So why not peer counseling? In this case, those who are not lonely can work with lonely teenagers in modeling for them how to initiate conversations, how to ask for dates, asking questions aloud, and so on. This peer reinforcement can help teach or guide lonely teenagers. If you are lonely, ask another teenager to help you in this area. If you are not lonely, then seek out a lonely teenager to help."

Peers who recognize a friend or acquaintance in need have several options available to lend support and assistance. Among them is making an effort to reach out and include that person in social activities. This can be as simple as inviting him or her to join your lunch table or study group. Away from school, inviting the person to a movie or a bowling night is a safe step. Or, invite the person over to your home to watch videos, which, because it's a relaxed environment, may be a more low-pressure social situation for someone who feels in the grip of loneliness and isolation.

Lending an Ear and a Helping Hand

People who want to help are told to see the world through the lonely person's eyes and try to imagine what he or she would want

Inviting a friend who is lonely to a night out is a great step in the direction of getting him or her back on track to a happy life.

done to help, then extend those acts to the friend. Lonely people have a lot on their minds and many ideas they might want to share, but they might not feel up to the task of conversation. Sometimes they just need a little push, a little invitation to start talking, and they may open up. So, if you know someone who is lonely, try to engage him or her in conversation, even if it isn't easy at first. Having lonely people share opinions and thoughts is a good first step in getting them past the emotions that are paralyzing them. You should be the listener, making them comfortable with what they have to say. Getting them to "talk out" their problem—or simply talk about anything at all—may be a huge step toward combating the loneliness.

As they begin to find their way out of their loneliness, you can help them create an action plan to keep the momentum going. Continue to listen and be encouraging. Let your friend make all the decisions for him- or herself. Offer guidance and

Strong friendships are the key to keeping loneliness at bay for the long term. You should always spend time with those who are most important to you.

advice, but don't take over the recovery process. Only the person suffering from loneliness can direct the process, and it is important for him or her to feel in control. You are there to support and assist at every turn.

If the loneliness is deep and prolonged enough, and you begin to feel you're in over your head, the time may have come to suggest that your friend seek professional help. In some ways, that may be the best help you can offer—a frank appraisal of your friend's situation and reassuring him or her that it is OK to seek such help. Make sure your friend knows that you will be at his or her side to lend whatever help or support will be needed now and in the future.

Glossary

alienation A withdrawing of one's affections from someone or something to which one was previously strongly attached.

antisocial Resistant to the company of other people; unsociable; hostile or harmful behavior.

anxiety A state of uneasiness and apprehension, as about future uncertainties.

clinical depression When a depressed person's condition worsens to the point where it interferes with the ability to function day to day and requires medical help.

depression A mood disorder represented by feelings of sadness, loneliness, despair, low self-esteem, withdrawal from interpersonal contact with others, and symptoms such as difficulty with sleep and a decreased or increased appetite.

disorientation Being displaced from a usual position or relationship; a feeling of having lost a sense of time, place, or identity.

existential Relating to earthly existence, to life; existence as rooted in time and space.

loneliness Feeling of deprivation resulting from unsatisfactory social relations with others. A feeling of isolation, alienation, or disconnectedness from others, often resulting in withdrawal from human contact.

peer An equal; someone of the same age, grade, or social group.

psychiatrist A medical doctor who specializes in the treatment of mental, emotional, or behavioral problems.

psychologist A mental health professional who studies the science of mind and behavior, and who offers counseling and therapy to patients.

self-esteem A confidence or satisfaction in oneself; self-respect.

suicide The intentional taking of one's life.

American Psychological Association (APA)

750 First Street NE

Washington, DC 20002-4242

(800) 374-2721

Web site: http://www.apa.org
   The APA's Help Center is an online resource for
   brochures, tips, and articles on the psychological issues
   that affect physical and emotional well-being, as well as
   information about referrals.

National Institute of Mental Health (NIMH)

Public Information and Communications Branch

6001 Executive Boulevard, Room 8184, MSC 9663

Bethesda, MD 20892-9663

(866) 615-6464

Web site: http://www.nimh.nih.gov
   The NIMH's mission is to reduce the burden of mental
   illness and behavioral disorders through research on
   mind, brain, and behavior.

StopLoneliness.com

ReconnectingU

P.O. Box 625

Reading, MA 01867

Web site: http://www.stoploneliness.com

StopLoneliness.com was developed by ReconnectingU, an organization dedicated to supporting the mental health and well-being of individuals as they move through their personal transitions. StopLoneliness.com is a clearinghouse of information and resources for people affected by loneliness.

Web Sites

Due to the changing nature of Internet links, Rosen Publishing has developed an online list of Web sites related to the subject of this book. This site is updated regularly. Please use this link to access the list:

http://www.rosenlinks.com/faq/lone

André, Rae. *Positive Solitude: A Practical Program for Mastering Loneliness and Achieving Self-Fulfillment.* New York, NY: Backinprint.com, 2000.

Carter, W. Leslie, Paul D. Meier, and Frank B. Minirth. *Overcoming Loneliness.* Grand Rapids, MI: Revell, 2000.

Copeland, Mary Ellen. *The Loneliness Workbook: A Guide to Developing and Maintaining Lasting Connections.* Oakland, CA: New Harbinger Publications, 2000.

Denkmire, Heather. *The Truth About Fear and Depression.* New York, NY: Facts on File, 2004.

Keena, Kathleen. *Adolescent Depression: Outside/In.* Lincoln, NE: iUniverse, Inc., 2005.

Lynch, James J. *A Cry Unheard: New Insights into the Medical Consequences of Loneliness.* Baltimore, MD: Bancroft Press, 2000.

Olds, Jacqueline, Richard Schwartz, and Harriet Webster. *Overcoming Loneliness in Everyday Life.* Secaucus, NJ: Carol Publishing Corp., 1996.

Pappano, Laura. *The Connection Gap: Why Americans Feel So Alone.* New Brunswick, NJ: Rutgers University Press, 2001.

Peck, Richard. *Strays Like Us.* New York, NY: Dial, 1998.

Piquemal, Michel, and Melissa Daly. *When Life Stinks: How to Deal with Your Bad Moods, Blues, and Depression.* New York, NY: Amulet Books, 2004.

Rylant, Cynthia. *The Islander.* New York, NY: Yearling, 1999.

Zucker, Faye, and Joan E. Huebel, Ph.D. *Beating Depression: Teens Find Light at the End of the Tunnel.* New York, NY: Franklin Watts, 2006.

Bernhardt, Stephen L. "Helping a Depressed Friend."
    Have-A-Heart.com. 1998. Retrieved May 5, 2006
    (http://www.have-a-heart.com/help-a-friend.html).

Brody, Jane E. "Personal Health." *New York Times* Online.
    April 6, 1983. Retrieved May 4, 2006 (http://query.
    nytimes.com/gst/fullpage.html?sec=health&res=
    940DE0D61139F935A35757C0A965948260).

"Coping Strategies." WebOfLoneliness.com. 2006. Retrieved
    May 2, 2006 (http://www.webofloneliness.com/
    coping_strategies.htm).

Fenton, Cathleen Henning. "Coping with Loneliness."
    About.com. December 2005. Retrieved May 2, 2006
    (http://panicdisorder.about.com/cs/loneliness/a/
    loneliness.htm).

Hitti, Miranda. "Loneliness May Drive Up Blood Pressure."
    WebMD. March 29, 2006. Retrieved May 2, 2006 (http://
    www.webmd.com/content/article/120/113804).

"How to Deal with Loneliness." University of Florida
    Counseling Center. November 2005. Retrieved May 2,
    2006 (http://www.counsel.ufl.edu/brochure.asp?include=
    brochures/how_to_deal_with_loneliness.brochure).

Keefe, Bill. "W.A.Y. Beyond . . . Loneliness." StopLoneliness.
    com. May 1, 2003. Retrieved May 2, 2006 (http://www.
    stoploneliness.com/).

Lear, Martha. "The Pain of Loneliness." *New York Times* Online. December 20, 1987. Retrieved May 4, 2006 (http://query.nytimes.com/gst/fullpage.html?res= 9B0DE4D7173EF933A15751C1A961948260&sec= health&pagewanted=print).

Lloyd, Robin. "Loneliness Kills, Study Shows." LiveScience.com. March 31, 2006. Retrieved May 2, 2006 (http://www. livescience.com/humanbiology/060331_loneliness.html).

"Loneliness." University of Cambridge Counselling Service. October 2003. Retrieved May 2, 2006 (http://www. counselling.cam.ac.uk/loneli.html).

"Loneliness." Wikipedia. Retrieved May 2, 2006 (http:// en.wikipedia.org/wiki/Loneliness).

"Loneliness and Isolation: Modern Health Risks." *The Pfizer Journal*. 2005. Retrieved May 2, 2006 (http://www. thepfizerjournal.com/default.asp?a=article&j=tpj15&t= Loneliness%20and%20Isolation%3A%20Modern% 20Health%20Risks).

"Loneliness Could Be in Your Genes." BBCNews.com. November 11, 2005. Retrieved May 2, 2006 (http:// news.bbc.co.uk/1/hi/health/4426184.stm).

Maleki, Meysa. "Loneliness." University of Toronto Counselling and Learning Skills Service. 2000. Retrieved May 2, 2006 (http://www.calss.utoronto.ca/pamphlets/loneliness.htm).

Marano, Hara Estroff. "The Dangers of Loneliness." PsychologyToday.com. August 21, 2003. Retrieved May 2, 2006 (http://www.psychologytoday.com/articles/ pto-20030821-000001.html).

Painter, Kim. "Loneliness Takes Its Toll." USAToday.com.
    April 24, 2006. Retrieved May 2, 2006 (http://www.usatoday.
    com/news/health/yourhealth/2006-04-23-loneliness_x.htm).
"Self-Help Brochures: Loneliness." Counseling Center at the
    University of Illinois. Retrieved May 2, 2006 (http://www.
    couns.uiuc.edu/brochures/loneline.htm).
"Types of Loneliness." WebOfLoneliness.com. 2006. Retrieved
    May 2, 2006 (http://www.webofloneliness.com/
    type_of_loneliness.htm).

Photo Credits

Editor: Nicholas Croce; **Series Designer:** Evelyn Horovicz
Photo Researcher: Amy Feinberg